# +Milklings+

**Sonya Wohletz**

***+Milklings+***


Edited by Brice Maiurro and Tyler Hurula



Books may be purchased in quantity and/or special sales by contacting the publisher. All inquiries related to such matters should be addressed to:

**South Broadway Press LLC**
1350 Josephine St Unit 102
Denver CO 80206

southbroadwaypress@gmail.com
www.southbroadwaypress.org
303.330.8083

First Paperback Edition, 2026
ISBN: 978-1-7350355-6-7
Library of Congress Control Number: 2026935400

Cover Art: Rachel Mulder
Cover Design: Brice Maiurro
Printed in the United States

## Praise for *Milklings*

"Milk. Colostrum. I am the first substance, the first miracle." Apparitions of the Mother Mary. Anesthesia. Risperidone. Daphne in the garden. In this brilliant sophomore collection, Wohletz erodes the false duality between the physical body and the divine. Through religious artifacts, human emotion, and the alchemical fluids of the birthing body, *+Milklings+* creates its own language and paradigm. To call this an elevation would be misleading—in the world of this collection, we are reminded of the divinity the body has always carried."

—Hailey Spencer, Author of *Glass Labyrinth*

"In her new collection, *+Milklings+,* Sonya Wohletz celebrates the physicality of birth and motherhood. With careful observation and precise language, the poems honor intimate, life-giving processes and the spirituality of the body. They draw us to consider the wonders of molecules and organs, then broaden the gaze to encompass the world. This collection makes physiology poetic. With its rich, intriguing language and unique imagery, it is an astonishing, wonderful read."

—Agnes Vojta, Author of *Love Song to Gravity*

"In Sonya Wohletz's *+Milklings+,* early motherhood reveals itself as the primal, chemical, and visceral season that it is, where women may find themselves "hung up to dry in the stirrups / like a storm-swollen door." Little of this language is soft, but it also resists turning harsh—instead, these poems erupt from a liminal space between "warm pearls of milk, cold pearls of salt." Reeling with the potential energy of uncorked champagne, *+Milklings+* melds science, history, ekphrasis, and experience to create a sanguine narrative of intuition and appetite."

—Erica Reid, Author of *Ghost Man on Second*

"Through its nerve network of images and sharp, tactile language, Sonya Wohletz's *+Milklings+* is an artifact of deep, intentional care. The metaphorical landscape is nearly cubist, how ideas and vocabularies rearrange themselves from poem to poem, giving the reader a new way to see. Motherhood is explored from the first person, but also turns outward toward myth, toward this contemporary moment in which the mother is at risk in every country. The forms, both inventive and anchored in tradition, paired with a docupoetic relationship to source, are demonstrative of the obsessive attention to the page reminiscent of Glück and Carson. Through its combination of textures, of weaving languages and themes, *+Milklings+* is a rhizomatic forest you don't immediately realize is a single tree, a collection creating oxygen to help you breathe."

—Wheeler Light, Author of *Blue Means Snow*

# +Milklings+

**Sonya Wohletz**

SOUTH BROADWAY PRESS
DENVER CO USA

## Contents

*For my children*

*De día y de noche*
*Quisiera tomar mi tetita*
*-Wendy Sulca*

# +I+

## Origins

Make vellum with these patagia,
a soft dark on softer

dark, the glans—tending apart
the rectos, then the versos;

pullulating the sloe-
eyed patience of the animals.

Where flesh meets flesh
the glitched-in vision recedes

and coalesces into the green singularity
at the center of rapture.

Whereas, along the periphery the jaw labors,
and the hands slow to a still as if closing a book.

Chaos purls—feathers
through new species—then, the last pull before

collapse—commands thumbs of salt
to become palms of sugar

çeşme başında

and the heaved tide rushes
to the tip of a budding moon,

and bursts the elements
of heaven open.

## Placentae

1.
Precision can save your life, or it can destroy
you according to its simple sequence—
one protein misplaced, over.

Vagary also has its promises, as in:
silken threads of a zygote—
twisting like algae in the tidal pool.

As in: where am I going amidst all this,
shuttled within
the violent grace
of a splayed cocoon?

Make no mistake—technique will get you noticed—
equally, it can help you arrive, undetected,
at the primordial spring,
if that is your preference,
to unspool the skein.

Consider the factors; evolve accordingly.

Root in and out of consciousness.
Bruise the womb's drupes or
loom them into fullness,
thirty and six strokes of the comb
along the banks of the purple river—

presently, a mouth will unhinge
at radical angles
to stitch the borders
along the edges of your suffering.

What is described within is not the same
as that which sustained you—

she is gone for good,
rooted beneath your memory.

2.
There was a thin mucosa
between you and I,
interspersed with the messengers
that fought the body's dominion.

All so that I might latch
and mutate—these four lobes:
my brothers and sisters—
each of you a planet, a dead moon,
a random debris—
you now arrange yourselves
into a novel coherence.

One side creates your wound;
the other side closes mine.

3.
Afterbirth—detachment—the open folio—
signaling the closed cloud—pour forth—
one vessel—through another—diverging in entropy—

4.
They took the mass in hand
like a maimed animal—
mule red against nitrile blue,
and prepared a burnt offering.

Steel sarcophagus or open grave:
can't you see?
I am losing faith.

5.
I could have eaten you,
as one eats the forest of new bones.

Each of their echoes:
sinister and hallow
like the pale sound of the bell
cast in the pit near the cathedral,
where all the workmen were left
to starve amongst each other.

I could have swallowed them all,
so as to stave my horror at the invasion.

6.
Better yet to have
buried you in the garden, amidst the cherry
and plum trees, the aphids and ants,
and the docile recognition
of earthworms.

7.
Why were you not born with a face
by which to properly mourn you?

In the mirror,
I see your zone of differentiation,
dividing in
shallow glass esters; a delta
shifting into a feast of reefs—

the thin ghost of your skin
touching mine,
cradling together our lost
bloods in separation.

## Let Down Reflex

Patterns are reflex—as anyone can observe:
dancers, thundering in shirrs of chaos
for a moment before they join hands.

There is, in these gestures, a physics of
trust—a theory of affinity that elides
description, yet imbues coherence to all action.

When you cleave the chert with your implements,
acknowledge how finely it fractures
the seabed for your sustenance.

In the same way, an infant—first,
not at all, and then all at once—
latches, sucks, and pulses with planet stem.

Notice the relations between
objects require, always, a certain syncopation,
unfurling in wheels of mounting oppositions:

the glands oscillating inside the storm,
their tensions percussed, stimulated
by the tongues of cold air currents;

the mosses beneath them
woven loosely along the inland
and then tighter along the shale-strewn shore,
furring the imprints of Ammonoidea.

When you break these fossils open, tell me
how the hemispheres match,
yet are somehow uneven.

Tell me about their drained sea.

Tell me the cells floating in this lymph
are not damned souls.

## Colostrum

Whatever they would have you believe,
the kept gods and
their powdery vocabularies,
stewing in commotions of unclear motive;

I am the first substance, the first miracle.

Not the skin on skin, the nurses hovering,
slapping, scraping, encasing.
Not the chemicals, slick and eager.
Not the satellite
of the doctor who retrieves his face
from the birth canal
and turns away.

Not even the mother, cloven and delicate;
nor the mouth's motions, which you
essayed so assiduously
those months in the floating realm.

Not the breath—
that which you already claimed as your own.

Rather, I arrive as your first visitor.
And like an apparition I swim briefly in your life,
my remedy proffered as opportunity:
take me in or don't.

While you dreamed it all—
I took up temporary
shelter in the host, like a *worme*
or an uncorked champagne.

I throat the pleasure of the toast,
for to oil the gravity
of your passage. To bless your necessity,

I fling myself through
the pleading innocence of your
tongue. I ply past the trap door
to your tiny, pea-sized stomach.

Thimble-cupped,
copper-balmed, syrupy
and simple. I seed
the notion of survival into form.

In the first days     you require
so little of me.
And in return, I relinquish
myself fully for you, in minute
slips and dribbles,
I give myself over
and then I vanish.

For you, who won't remember my taste.
For you, who hold the missiles and the missives
whole within your own mouth
and sink the weight of oceans in your refuse.

And yet
I like to think of it like this—
You slip me free of the last generation.
And thus I don't concentrate my power in endings—

I, the original elixir,
sating all who permit my liminal solitudes.

**Milk Coming In**

The sky breached in early morning;
called out for instruction amidst great confusion.
And the panes of glass
in their lapsed laminae,
speckled with mold—

still had no reason to respond back,
no reason but the reflection.

I was like a doll there, a broken record,
a repeating refrain, a series of sleepless nights.
I could be splayed apart on the table,
my folds examined for anomalies—
sutured, or torn accordingly.

Believe me when I tell you
there were no extravagances.
The gestures were all calculated, predictable;

I could be plastered to the bed,
cradled within a vinyl wedge,
or rolled between billable stations—
the degrees and timing of these
locutions made no difference.

And of course,
everyone grew tired of me (even the nurses)—
my blank eyes, my heavy portage,
the catheter of my tongue swirling
around the same syllables yet
producing no meaning.
My skin a plastic bladder,
its void,      could be carried like a purse.

Anything could happen and it wouldn't
surprise or distress the others,

least of all me.
So I signed my own confessions.

I thought I looked best then,
swaddled in synthetic robes, scratched
by a false breeze,
or hung up to dry in the stirrups
like a storm-swollen door
buckling in its strained frame—
impossible to open and therefore
impossible to leave through. And so

other plans had to be devised—a false account,
a house sale, a poultice of cabbage leaves,
a letting loose of dogs once deemed sacred.

Don't read these lines and think me hard
or bitter—the change was only momentary—
three days at most. If it registered at all,
it can be corrected still, retroactively—
like any specious account.

If I hurt you,
please know
it was only because
there was no one else there to warn you,
no one else to seal the hungers.

## Early Spring

Early spring arrives like a razor
to gut the clouds, their fluid light
dripping along the seams of shadows.

In the garden the red soil pulses,
holding in its fist
tough knobs—
the bulbs of an old life.

Eventually it must also relinquish this
to the wide plate of the sun.

The energy required is enormous.

Bleats incessantly, though
goes on ignored, as do
most important actions.

And yet the night freezes arrive
new and dangerous—exacting their
bite into the walls of the house,
the jugular pipes seizing, stuttering
predictions about
the family cycle inside.

In early spring
it feels somehow useless
to thaw.

Time leaks in from behind
dusty panes of rage
and stalls on the sills.

Only at this moment and no other
does ritual present itself as decision:
whether one takes

the bladed crocus in hand,
or is rather taken
under its purple flag.

The colorlessness below: an outcome
that signals the
preparation of the garden
for new children, new autumns.

Above:
mother and son are still whirring together.

The breadth of her armspan
articulates the limits of her imagination.

What she describes as a means to comfort—
the light returning northward,
the crocuses blooming beneath the apple tree,
the ice, thawing into blurred puddles—

these, he experiences only as an expression of the superficial.

One day he will circle beyond that embrace.
In the reflection
of his dark eyes:
the promise of her burial.

But always there is the procession,
the bright wings of air,
the sensation of weight taking up again
the arthritic argument of a new return.

One sun closer to my death
my voice devises
fuller colors as adversary.

Watch, it rises.

**Foremilk/Hindmilk**

Creation is endurance, in a sense.
Where there is great thirst, one must learn temperance.

The first sounds flow,
sputtering, overwhelming, whole.

And that which contained them (with no great ease)
shudders with pleasure at the release.

But for anything to properly extend,
the thirst is first something with which one learns to contend.

The volumes of those early images and signs—
their fluid abundance floods the mind.

With patience, one learns to take them as a signal,
not as fulfillment of the initial

need, but rather as a means to prepare
for a deeper density in awareness.

It is either the beginning of a dream
or a waking alchemy.

# +II+

## Risperidone

*Risperdal blocks dopamine's action on the pituitary gland and can cause the levels of prolactin to increase and reach abnormal levels. In women, prolactin stimulates breast development and breast milk production.*[1]

*Galactorrhea is a well-known adverse drug reaction (ADR) of numerous antipsychotic drugs (APD) and is often distressing for those affected (Glocker et al., 2021).*[2]

What can I tell you
that could alter everything you knew in me?
An image, perhaps, rather than any words.
If I manage to conjure it,
would you forgive my defects, my diagnosis?

With your permission, I have something you may like:

There is a scene of the old apartment
in the Irish Channel, before the hurricane:
a young woman, crying again in the bathroom
because the man she thinks she loves
doesn't understand that *play* means
you still have to follow certain rules,
not your own urge for violence.

As she weeps, pearls of milk condense
upon her round and rigid nodes.

This milk:
in spite of the fact that there is no
(and never will be)
baby to speak of between them:

---

[1] Mayo Clinic Connect, "Risperidone caused me to lactate and stopped my period." https://connect.mayoclinic.org/discussion/risperidone-caused-me-to-lactate-and-stopped-my-period/. Comment from Amanda Roe, 19 December 2021. Accessed 21 March 2025.

[2] Glocker C, Grohmann R, Engel R, Seifert J, Bleich S, Stübner S, Toto S, Schüle C. Galactorrhea during antipsychotic treatment: results from AMSP, a drug surveillance program, between 1993 and 2015. Eur Arch Psychiatry Clin Neurosci. 2021 Dec;271(8):1425-1435. doi: 10.1007/s00406-021-01241-3. Epub 2021 Mar 25. PMID: 33768297; PMCID: PMC8563638.

Warm pearls of milk, cold pearls of salt:
of course, they are beautiful,
especially against a nude backdrop.
And the man's body does slack
as the liquids enter his awareness.

For twenty-four years I had a body,
and I had a mind—like a chemical bath.
I splashed in it; I cleansed myself in it
from time to time,
and then I drowned.
When I emerged, it became apparent—
the function of my breasts, their tremulous volumes,
their sensorium of purpose yet to be ful-
filled.

If the pills gave me anything
it was this false sense,
not a nutritive lactation, but rather like
the resinous tears adorning
the polychrome
sorrow of a dolorous virgin.

Both substances (the pills and the tears):
a sign of suffering, disguised as moral achievement.

Yet, I can understand, no man
could resist this alternative gloss:
the milk, the tears,
their art upon the female form—
how could they be anything
other than the product
of his insistent hands alone?

But I slipped those ivory lozenges in my throat,
And still I failed to silence the screaming knife
inside my brain.

So take this image from me,
as if you were to take a cure:

the wet light of a shattered star,
leaking through the woman—its liquids
collecting on the flesh;
they never reach the floor.

## Catatonia Girl

*After Adriana Paredes Pinda*

*Sóplame un canto sencillo y duradero*

Comadrona de mil nudos—
extendiendo tus lenguas como azogues
de luz por el espacio para predicar
la salvación de los vientres perdidos,
encarcelados in the halls of a hospital,
las visiones en ceremonia de laurel
para mostrar a los pecadores que
la mujer solitaria no finge sus cuerpos,
no finge sus mil fuegos, sus aires
brotando en los pulmones de vidrio,
el útero, estómago, estado—carie de caridad—
ya nadie te puede alcanzar.

[They cut our tongues so we wouldn't speak]

We had no music for it, just these
ingots of plastics to mend the throats,
parasites embedding the slack muscles, the pilled salt,
columnas girding the black lobes
of concrete, our enclosure, our forsaken virtues.

[The mind black and empty, a winking abscess]

We open our mouths, but not in
anticipation of your prescribed prayers—
qué los doctors nos bendigan
qué no nos pronuncien muertas
that the diagnosis fits your clinical training
qué mis leches no nos condenen
to a servitude of hidden skills, of learning
to live with the disease of profound distrust.

Quiero saber si mi lengua te da miedo
o si a lo mejor te nutre, si te sostiene, mis propias
leches flinging into the air like wings,
coming apart and condensing together again,
como espectáculos de vapores fulgentes,
the fungi of the air filtration device,
its system of lengthy collapse.

o si el sabor de mi silencio te contenta—
my hair lank, my eyes glazed,
performing well the docile patient
who wheels into the hallway without complaint.

She wants to know—mujer de la sala de urgency,
si el propósito de vivir
te amanece con la misma gravedad, gris, sour—
como las mareas del insólito ayer,
o si de una vez you tripped in those wires—

her scars, do they tie your own mouth shut,
her limp, soft tongue, was it
taken for the newest pet after the assessment.

## The Amethyst

Your eager blade cracked through me, and I fractured
in the sun's commerce; before, there
was the crushing comfort of my velvet habitat,
the warm scent of earth feathering inside itself.

And not knowing time, I chaliced it,
blue-sluiced, molecule by molecule,
to morpheme into what you see now—a body

schismed by a strange order—
the pitted, fractalled heart, these cold, cloistered bones,
planulae for a tongue, blading the light.

Experience has taught me: heat and pressure
kill independent thought, but still the voice
endures, multisyllabic and crystalline, though
it will only speak in one color; predictable,
like a womb—
I find myself for sale everywhere.

And I am told that humans desire
to possess history almost as much
as they desire possession of riches: for
both purposes, the Greeks cut
goblets from my hips
to stave their addiction—
the depths of the seas, the violet swallows.

Do you think you can subordinate me to
your energetic needs when you haven't
understood the praise of your own poisons?

Still, I recall the taste of ancient wine
slicing in my teeth—
dark and syrupy with manure, blood,

and resin. Nothing that could kill your modern cravings;
its meaning has slipped your vessel.

But I’m hard, and equal to it;
and perhaps that is your saving grace.
If an enemy steals into the home,
grab hold of me and strike.

## In Those Days

In those days there was a way to understand things.
It was simple—for instance,
if the man glanced back
as he retreated beyond the fence,
it meant he was not your father.
Or, if a message arrived when your thinking
achieved a peak of concentration, it
meant the sender could be shaped.

Concentration. In those days
it could be summoned, inhaled like smoke.
The world, in its availability, attended it.

Only then could I arrange
the future. A series of actions bereft of image.

Or perhaps the image
(for one time only)
entered inside its fullest being,
blank and possible,
and called to me in familiar ways.

**Swallow**

Even the pill on the tip of your tongue is afraid
of what happens in the dark.

Caught between a glottal stop
and tongue to palate pause—

pinked folds where salivary methods dissolve the
firmly formed remark, or

regrets multiply in millions,
all oblong-membraned and not at all special.

Their moment was an hour ago, or perhaps
we all broke down

the complex symmetry of their false sugars,
The rudiments of laboratory. A

heat duct for a womb, soft asbestos swaddling.
Formica footprints migrating

beyond the threshold where clouds and
children stretch arms out wide as fences,

*neverminding* the medicines we take.

## Does Not Own It

1.
It is not so much the low fix of the sky,
but the rain and the sound the rain makes against
the metal roof—plangent and singular
like an apology.

And the earth beyond the hollow reply
is a swollen canker sore—
stings with each plea for resurrection.

2.
In the first garden
it must have been warm
even beneath the ribbons of rain that sheltered it.

The earth rolled smoothly in that great vacuum
knowing only the comfort of its own ferrous
viscera pluming within
like a parasite—

and the punishing scorn of radiation, which was constant,
and thus accepted.

3.
Now and then,
the woman dresses—first the two small children—
and then herself
in tired garments
that hang against their gaunt spines
like scripture.

She ushers them forth
from the grease-stained hovel,
the door behind them closing
wet, with sleeves of winter rain.

Behind it,
the man tunnels out a code,
impenetrable though predictable—

he does not
know his own thirst.

4.
Rivering through the morning,
faint molecules merge and divide
precisely and according to their kind.

Conversations about the weather,
the mending of clouds
across the deserted plot, these among
the things we have in common.

They, too, can ply their wares—
the slithered organs,
all asking,
all waiting, waiting.

Thirst is their expedient.

5.
If she thinks that the water
remembers less than her,
she will drown,
surely
she will drown,
a mere seed
of withered earth
for a lung.

6.
Now the rain holds the earth as in
a false matrix, promising something solid
that it, itself, fears—

but what the water knows
does not own it.

## Sexed and Fed Wet Candy

I sometimes feel like a woman
at the pool—good example
and like a good woman I know
where to find the curtains
|nude w/lockerroom|

If you are asking—*please tell me you are asking*—
Yes, they match (but someday won't)

Then the priest whistles his treacles at me

but I forgot—he isn't a real priest,
just a lifeguard, a young man
red shorts & tank top
tasked to mind that I don't drown
in blue whoreyness

While he does that—representational drift—
unisex hammam
|timestamp: bubblegumSnickersSwedish-fish|
break time/shift change:
the lifeguard girlies in cropped tops
and flitting breasts
and like good girls they'll know
how to find the screens
|digital synapse|
|blocksafety|

Meanwhile I'll keep to my floundering
waters without desire
though my cervix still sheds light

like kerosene
my breasts—
slack and purposeful, tuggable |juice*purrs*inme|

When I was younger, I knew myself
only as male desire,
which means, I felt like a man:
lumbering my thick thighs
through the humid lane of
another man's gaze

|outofwater|

I could imagine pleasure then
a dreamed re-entry
falling capsule through
slippery skins
spits of oxygen

|manmodule|

First, external: assessing the earth like an antique krater
then
internal: smashing the whole display
with one flick of a falling eyelash,
flaming through bruised ropes of cloud,
the ocean for a tongue,
sexed and fed with wet candy
abandoning fear of rescue

# +III+

## Prolactin

1.
When something ends, heaves off,
or departs, the body mourns—
even if the senses cannot follow its subtler motions.

Perhaps the eyelids thicken, or the heart slows,
floating like a pale anemone in crystal waters,
the right atrium taking in
oxygen only passively,
as the low tides of blood
slide through it
towards richer, more potent territories.

And the natural appetites wane—so, too,
their mineral consequences: the bone
lacquer dimming, the tiny red vesicles rolling through
the arteries, then the veins, into
the palace of the lungs,
burning like a golden horde—
then bruising into faint blue
halos like those of suffering
martyrs digging
their shriveled hopes into the permafrost.

Blunting and darkening
until they appear more a natural
cousin of the microplastics
that swarm the ducts
like peripatetic merchants.

2.
When I gave birth and parted
with your purple robes of placenta,
I understood the true meaning of the word
*vulnerability*. Not only as an inherent symptom of
the human condition upon entering the

world, but as the only way in which
one finally opens to it—

and thus learns to live as separate from ideals
like immortality, or wisdom.

In the span of a few hours,
I saw these replaced
by a physical language,
a body without organs—

torn flesh, Pitocin, the numbness
of endurance—wound gaping
in the exhausted husk—chemicals
synthesizing through the synapses,
as if reviving an ancient aqueduct.

Then, cradled
within the ruins of me,
my son opened his dark eyes
to take in the impression of
the world thrumming in its vernix—

Outside, the season's
forest fires erected columns of
opaline smoke to mount the vault
of a scarlet August moon.

The night's gate then opened,
and the body reappeared beyond its margins,
as if it had finally found a way
to claim a new expression—
a lion roaring through our wilderness.

## Madonna Lactans

*After a painting by Mateo Pérez de Alesio, 1590*
*Oil on wood panel*
*33 x 44 cm*
*Fundación Pedro y Angélica de Osma*
*Lima, Perú*

1.
The woman's hooded eyes
slope downward from within
a dark context—a whisper of gauze
veils the clarity of her vision.

She coils her attention around the infant form.
He, unperturbed, meets our gaze and
reaches confidently for the breast.

2.
I drift in warm pools of parallax.
The baby, there, beside me peaceful
and solid like an oak panel. My mind
wraps itself in black silk,
the voices, receded—
as if to seek their sustenance elsewhere.

3.
The woman in the picture exposes her left breast,
its flesh still micaceous and smooth,
and strings the nipple like an arrow in its bow.

The child lays his hands on her as upon
a bowl of raw clay
shaping its supple essence
to the curving form of his palms.

4.
When I used the pump to try to increase
my supply, I often suffered.

I needed the warm water from the shower
and urgent massages to loosen the frequent clogs.
I worked and squeezed through the burning pain
until I could see the bulging duct—the culprit,
like an enemy erupting from deep within
my chest. I thought I needed strawshard
to pierce the disturbance.
But then I would summon the latch
and burst flesh between my fingers
into a thin stream of relief,
draining two days' worth of trapped milk,
a wing blooming in the wrong direction.

5.
The painter prepares the surface first, planing,
sanding, burnishing. And then layers the thin
skins of gesso—the sticky essence of the earth—
marble dust, water, and hide glue. After it dries, he
conjures form: a young mother and her infant son.

They bloom in rosy gradients of azuritas, cal viva,
bermellones, oropimente, albayalde, and cochinilla.

Then he clothes the pigments
with the textures of time.

6.
These are the intimacies
of art, that they may pollinate
your good health.

7.
Once the conditions were met,
the iconography secured,
the earth mined open,
I held your raw church like a jaw
and her myth boiled through me
becoming meadow, a blue basin of stone,

a ripe cloud approaching
to quench the depths of your system.

## Ada at the Breast

1.
My child is at my breast;
she gazes at the contrasting
pattern of my shirt.

Light purling unto ellipses,
the gravitational axis
netting the textured ache—

I release
this involuntary universe
from my body,

eyes
narrowing,
widening.

She clasps her cold hands,
humming as warm
milk churns
in her mouth.

2.
It is not the way
the world wants us,
you and I;

red cheek pressing
against my alluvial veins,
snaking jade rivers
roiling through this
once familiar landscape—

hair falling,
belly expanding,
milk leaking,
legs smoothing, softening
as the head lifts and cries, oh—
the miles I ran
now a still frame—

all those strivings between one tall road
and the shallow arroyo,
sand swallowing
the softly padded soles,
then south;

a eucalyptus grove opening
to the equatorial anvil of the sky
and yellow grasses grazing
westward on the Pajarito plateau.

This body burning itself into nothingness,
into what it wanted of nothingness.

And so I drifted,
my body
blaring its siren
through fires, then
dozing in blankets of embers.

I took the ashes
in palmfuls
and painted my fingernails with the pitch
of a diseased forest.

I held these offerings in my
thirst
and drank in deeply,
each chemical scorch
a mouthful of salt,
the pillars beckoning—admonishing.
What am I but the gazing past of ancestors
remembering what they could not,
forgetting what they could not?

And then I felt you;
your whole body a course of action—
shapes this clay of care between
mother and infant—

Infant
Infant

Daughter

You are smiling at me now, my mercy,
mercy of the world,
your body—safe with mine.

3.
Cold grey arches its smooth belly over
the low glades of Puget sound.
A cherry tree huddles beneath the weight
of its accumulated mosses,
brittle branches, twigs—
lichened, ant-trailed, and
whiskered with fungi, knows the seasons,
strokes them with its long roots.

Far below the wet decay:
the horizons we cannot penetrate.

Ancient fragments parceled;
each chain of starch and polyphenols
seeping lower,
one phrase further to the xylem.

4.
New stems urge skyward,
the gnarled bits piercing between
these questions that flow—

a golden milk
that cannot articulate its way
yet into language.

5.
You and I have made it through this dark winter,
shouldering the weight of an empty village.

We gather it in around
like folds of a thick blanket—
the same pattern I felt knitting within me
those long months.

And you paused
my staggering thoughts
continued
emerging
from within the weft
of this ancient gift—

6.

CH3-(CH2)7-CH=CH-(CH2)7-COOH CH3(CH2)14COOH MicroRNA linolcic/alphalinolenic acids IgA, IgG, IgM epidermal growth factor
lysozyme immunoglobulin A caseinfolate-binding protein bifidus factor lipase amylase PRP alpha1-antitrypsin antichymotrypsin haptocorrin CH3-(CH2)7-CH=CH-
Pb/Ca/P/Mg/I/Se/Cu/An/Na+/K+/C+ staphylococcusstreptococcus lactobacillus Propionibacterium A/B1/B2/B6/B12/D cytokines/chemokines alpha-lactalbumin
terminal Gal-(beta1,4)-Glc GNF/CNIF/HNF/adiponectin/IGF/IGF-1/2/NGF/Epo glutamine macrophage stem cell
docosahexaenoic acid disaccharide lactose oligosaccharides saccarides/saccarides/saccarides secretory IgA lactoferrin leukocytes

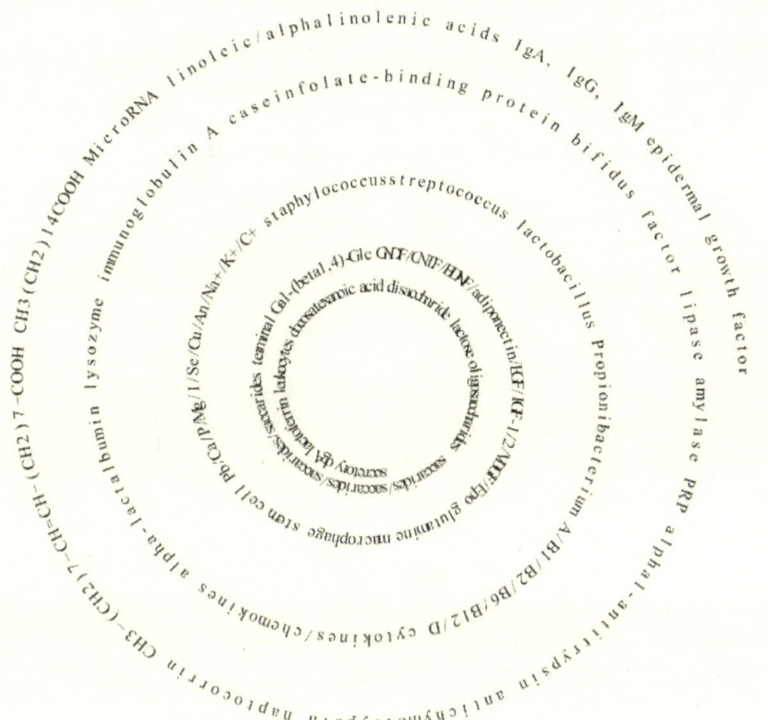

7.
She wove this for us,
some long ago mother that I still need,
that you still need.

She grieved
those who could no longer cry out for nourishment.

As she wove and the cold air burned.

As she starved,
her breath short,
yet steady,

and her breasts withered.

One more trip into the icy wind
to gather in the felled branches
that burn on the darkest nights,
their cherry smoke
curling in a tight grip of awareness
around the throats of the would-be killers

ranging just beyond the furthest hillock.

8.

Yes, let this feral urge comfort us—
her milk courses through
sweet with the songs of survival.

## Apparition of the Virgin to Saint Bernard

*After a painting by Bartolomé Esteban Murillo, c. 1655*
*Oil on canvas*
*311 cm x 249 cm*
*Museo del Prado*
*Madrid, Spain*

*Fly with thine eyes all round about this garden;*
*For seeing it will discipline thy sight*
*Farther to mount along the ray divine.*
-St. Bernard speaking in Dante Alighieri, *Paradiso*, Canto XXXI

Since I suppose it's my life's
calling to follow some kind of order,
you can find me ensconced in my books, studying,
sending emails, arranging problems for
the sake of solving them—

I didn't foresee
the garden of your breasts
arching to rescue me—

woman with a fork for a brain,
woman who moves mouth-deep
through vitreous humor,
imagination thronged with venus flytraps—
none of your analytic powers will serve you.
You're asleep again, aren't you? Because the world
won't correspond your visions.

What are you seeking from my picture?
Some enlightenment or insight
as to why you turned out the way you did?
Try tasting instead.

If you want that, you'll have to move your tongue
around in a certain way, not rest

your chin on my foot, waiting
for a stranger to feed you.

You've learnt nothing
from these books but obedience—
your first language—which is also
the language of grief.

The second would be the language of instruction:
wherein, one seeks to elide the institution
through the subjugation of others.

The third will be a slackening of the jaw,
while you predicate blank
legajos to the mortal eyelids;
dissolution of servitude,
diffusion of preference—
a kind of recognition
that doesn't require fixed attention.

My relief
will then descend from the inlaid folds
of the mounting clouds—
the cherubs underfoot, then more clouds, of course,
then more cherubs.

The four walls of your study
will disperse, its varnishes
will blur into shadows,
playing open the chromium
iris of dawn—

a perception that does not perceive
its own glazing rhythms.

## Our Lady of Lost Appetites

1.
At her shrine (bathroom mirror after the first shower in days),
I offer a votive of empty images:

> *oatmeal-pasta-peanut-butter-cookies-fresh-bread-and-butter-fish-shrimp-clams-berries-flax-seed-avocado-beans-and-rice-cherry-juice-raisins-dried-apricots-bone-broth-lentils-pumpkin-seeds-yogurt-cheese-(lots of cheese)-cornmeal-ground-beef-with-spices-cinnamon-cumin-paprika-pine-nuts-eggplant-tomatoes-in-olive oil-more-cookies-hot-chocolate-melons-enchiladas-more-cookies-cheetos-chips-pizza-more—*

2.
I light a candle (cropped wick of grace) and stare back at what confronts me—the raw marble of the belly— the vague abdominals frayed at the seams like cheap elastic; within, the uterus urging itself to station back into the confusion of what was once a pelvis, a dimpled saddle of thighs thundering their forced cadence, the thinned hair, folding like a wimple across the sallow forehead, the breasts, unrecognizable in their new girth—the dish-sized nipples, darkening stars signaling their red shifts from a distant galaxy—

3.
For years, I sought perfection in an emptiness
that anchored my life like a stone
to the silence of an arroyo
before the threat of flash flood—

total purgation.

All through this mute penance,
I tried to discern blessing vs. punishment
(there was no caul).

But, as the saints admonish—
there is no way to distinguish
the self through penance;
there is only the commitment
to repetition,
the *over and over* of *over and over*,
until desire transforms
via the rudimentary pressures into
a rote memory that stands in
for what in other contexts,
you might call *indifference*.

Maybe this is the only way to stay alive.

Or maybe it is only a reflection,
a mocked-up purgatory,
something worth practicing while you can—

the flames burn for a while,
though for how long exactly, nobody can say.

4.
I am aching for something
I want to call renewal;
a voice—or perhaps

a radical form
emerging from the hot steam
of these ablutions
as if from behind
a veil that lifts
from the village
icon on a feast day
to bless and cure all lost causes:

> *All practice requires*
> *simplicity:*

*Take it easy on the nuts, the chile,*
*and the garlic to keep*
*your milk tasting nice!*

*Also, no mint, no sage.*

*Everything else—make a habit*
*to savor, girl,*

*and remember:*
*the image is allowed*
*its own species*
*of equivocation.*

# +IV+

## One Species Thin (November 2024)

I tuck my children in bed every night
and tell them stories

Sometimes they are the same stories
though they may be repeated

as if to double weave
the dark village anew

But there are always variations—whether
in the tone or inflection of the voice

syllables coldly settling each molecule
into fresh puddles of sound

or, the telling may be graveled with exhaustion
motoring and choric

The story shifts as my
children hinge and angle

elbow bounce and giggle—reach to swirl
their fingers towards the feral hiss of the page

pulling at my shirt in that familiar request that makes flow
the elemental syrups of my breasts all stories

nourishing their neural newness
the wandering vibration pulse

parting through the buttery cortex
small spark into colorless grove—

their eyes parsing
implicating fresh hues of blood from within

the shaded hemisphere, dopaminergic
blooms in rhythm with the supple

beings that shiver
into the equanimity of their own fur

Later: the equation of the mother tongue against
the young as they cry out mineral in the night

to exhume anew—
the texture of confusion thinning away, now

one species removed
from the shoals of our fabled slumber

## Cueva de Murciélagos

Voy caminando
bajo un cielo rojo, y la penumbra falla
(the sky was flat, unyielding
into its wish for darkness—
this throat of mine
fastened into
the lid of the blue world)
Aquí mi sombra no
se detiene en las pausas del pavimento
ni se estremece frente a la orilla
de aguas corrientes,
frías y llenas de cenizas mudas
(moments that you
never knew how to sing
to me)
paralelas que van entre un ojo al otro—
la mano subida, esperando su
turno para luchar.
(or caress,
which for the child—
no lesson can bear
recollection)
No te voy
a callar, ni me vas a pedir
que cante.
Oh, gato,
(curled into the cave
of the mouth
as in question)
reina de mi niñez
causa de mis anhelos, por
dónde te fuiste cuando se invirtió
la luna sobre mi voz? Esperas,
(a memory approaches,
softly stalking its prey)

apenas, un mordisquito para
aplacarte, o talvez te hiciste
amiga del murciélago,
mensajero del inframundo. Lloro por
sus promesas dulces y finas

(the night inverted
as promised,
though flightless)

como tus besos en la frente cuando
brote mi confusión
otra vez.

(as I named you
the words shifted
into the shape
of their own habitat)

los susurros corren por la cueva
de esta voz, suspendido entre
las gotas del ayer
y el humo animal de mi pensar.

## General Anesthesia

Not the breath, clapping against bales of flesh.
Not the mountain, placating the sky for elevation.
Not the winter, abstracting.
Not words, not sounds,

not their syndicates,
but the ceiling, shimmering with black warrants
while the doctor counts down from five into the veins,
opens and closes the body in a memory
that refuses availability.

So similar, it seems now—
the day a woman and a man met
and lifted the night in their weak hands
before opening together an enemy spine.

A new Eden, darkens—

Not the breath taking up residence
along the circuits and sutures.

not the structure,
but the emptiness between vertebrae.
A shadow box—
this serpent among the branches
clicking its husk inside the
joints for each missed puncture.

## Ascites

1.
The mornings of illness accumulated
in swelling globes of light within your belly.
As though you were gravid with miracle,
as though the miracle held illumination.
It was a strange vision
for your youngest, who had never witnessed
you with child—the body full—
a sign of the unrealized efforts now
turned inward;
to you, reclined in your hospital bed,
like a single white calla lily
lain against raw linen, your ample
petals tapered to the simple
stem of your exhausted form.
The exudate serum imprisoned within,
protein-rich and heady. Its message—
incomprehensible, no satin tongues,
no furnace to touch its origin.

2.
How could you not understand?
You heard my cries of pain,
smelled the chemicals in my puke.
Were you not moved?
Though it is true: certain things can't be
argued by the dying. As for the living—
they won't dare guess at
the caverns of experience
held within the body,
couching the organs as in
a field of dark matter.
I wanted you to see it that way,
and measure it back to me; perhaps then
I could have accepted this suffering, or
perhaps you could have.

Either way,
I couldn't read your absent expression.
Lack of comprehension, I suppose, stands as its own
witness to the accusation of independence.
Only when I realized that could I finally
reach into myself for my own mother.
Dead now forty years, I held her gently
in my abdomen and we receded together.

3.

A young woman watches from the foot of the bed as the nurses perform paracentesis, draining the fluid from its carnal sack. The patient—beyond her body—closes her eyes, her face serene. And the nacreous fluids shine now as they join their glass houses beside the bed.

4.

-The patient is supine, awake and alert

-The ascitic fluid level is percussed to perform a paracentesis

-16 G angiocath is inserted at 45 degrees 4 cm superomedial to the anterior superior iliac spine (without imaging guidance), using z-tracking technique to minimize the chance of an ascites fluid leak

-Approx. 4 L of fluid removed from the peritoneal cavity

-Patient received 50 cc of albumin IV (25% solution) over 2 hours

-Patient reports reduced intra-abdominal pressure and relief of associated dyspnea

5.

In this view, it is important to note—the proportions are skewed: the girl is larger than in real life, and the glass bottles—much smaller.

(The contents:
like terror or love—
await their own proof
in extraction)

## Formula

Because I never knew your taste as an infant,
I offer a formula of returns:

The mixtures you used to sustain me
(because progress, then, required extinction of instinct)

These are the chemistries we used to sustain you;
the parabola of the jejunostomy, its sacks of succor—

Yet, I am grateful for them;
the human designs that permitted those bonds.

Therefore, I declare a balance to the equation
to honor the dignity(x) of (y)our being.

## Bilirubin

*After Luci Tapahonso*

1.
My mother sits on the porch in the afternoon sunlight
and opens the top buttons of her cotton blouse
to expose her rind to the sun.

With some effort, she reclines in her chair. A moan escapes
and then settles into the breeze through piñón trees.

I am beside her, like an itch.
My thoughts range the folds of my own flesh
and find no peace.

She raises her slender, yellow hand,
to shade her eyes and gazes at me:

I see it now, there is recognition
in recollection, and the salts pool in the humors
as the body stalls, its rivers dammed.

2.
When the baby is breastfed exclusively
you need to expect jaundice,
because the liver
can't yet break down
the extra red blood cells.

The skin will
pitch to a new palette,
iodine-like and electric.

And the whites of the eyes
will swerve to new harmonics.
When they open from sleep,
you will lose yourself
in their opacity and think back;

the errors suddenly evident,
the guilt, firmly established
in warm inks.

Then, the urine darkens. You watch
for signs of dehydration, counting wet diapers.
But the pigments remain, adamant and frightening;
they can endure for months.

3.
For today, at least,
quell your alarm;
the baby is alert, alive.

4.
The mother, on the other hand,
curls away, as within a still life.
You can see the vivid tint of her,
evoke her essence, but her
presence remains in memory,
as albedo.

5.
I brushed your long dark hair
and saw in your eyes, for the first time,
the faint whisperings of your death. When
you asked if I recognized these colors, I couldn't
distinguish them; my language blocked—beside the tumor,
bloated like a fish in the receding tide,
to which no remedy concedes comfort.

6.
The baby bestows her
first smile (around two months);

share salt with your relatives,
salt and laughter. It irises
the tongue, to have a baby among you.

7.
When the moon rises again,
archaic and alone,
how I will know its yellow spectacle
as anything other than illusion:
as atmospheres osmosing a disarray of
sick light; as the sun reporting
its own dying over and over,
to a diorama of rocks and gasses, inert?

8.
There is the familiar song, Juan Luis Guerra,

intonating intoxication: me sube la bilirrubina cuando te miro y no me miras.

If you move your limbs in a certain way,

maybe you forget them for a while,

maybe you slide between gazes—

or, you take the unspoken lesson from the song:

admit to no symptoms. The evidence

stains itself onto the afflicted, in any case.

9.
Let the moon metabolize these visions—
there is no way
to absolve them otherwise.

10.
That way, the baby will sleep and grow,
immune to the suffering of the dead.

11.
You may find yourself yet
dressing in the skins of
a new life.

As shield, as shroud—
evaporating
in brilliant and dangerous wavelengths,
invisible to the naked eye.

**For Sally**

*I will tell you about your grandmother, Johnnie,*
she said in a Southern accent.

As she spoke, I crouched down
into the entrance of a bookstore on Oak Street,
as if to occult myself beneath
its station of broken blocks,
thumbing the waxy beads in prayer—
the necklace she gifted me for my twenty-seventh birthday.

*Your grandmother was quiet,* she said,
*except when she was around her sisters.*
Laughing in the kitchen, red nails darting,
smoke braiding the dark colors of those years—
(she didn't know then, those were her middle years).

That was over half a century ago, my mother
an only child of the marriage that forced
Johnnie north to cold lakes and a blizzard of suburbs,
to the bruising scorn of her husband's addiction.

Years later, a photograph in the mail:
*She cut the cake at our wedding reception*
*Almost 50 years ago 5/31/1975.*

*Your mother was also there with a good friend at the house afterward—*
*but we were on our way to our honeymoon.*

*It seems not all that long ago...*
*until I look in the mirror!!*

*Now it is off to Italy with my college friends, after that, will*
*conduct breast cancer surgeon surveys at three hospitals,*
*then to Louisville to see our granddaughters.*

3/22/25

Dear Sally,

How many times have you looked at the trees in spring and admired their spare and intelligent branches? Their icy blossoms, priming to nectar the insects. So similar to mammary glands—do they seem that way to you, too? A map for sucrose and sunlight. Now you map stories of women and hold their memories. Your incisive gift to prune what needs pruning and save what needs saving.

## Memorial

*For Martha*

1.

The idea of heaven, like the real thing—
being only *a posteriori*—

or perhaps described best in the
bureaucratic terms, *after the fact*,
like a government contract,
slow to execute, and minimal only
in its remunerative capacity.

A shining, slippery
thing with an inflated
sense of its own importance—
like the white of a blank page,
or the eyes rolled back in the head;
an aberrant, liminal state,
promising equally, and without prejudice:
ecstasy, horror,
or despondency.

Or, as in the case of the contract:
something whose terms can easily be redrawn,
redirected according to whim.

2.

When you were an infant, if you gazed up
you didn't see the sky.
Nor did you see the wings of the purported
angels swan diving to join you in your pram—
like virgins on the funeral pyre
of a great monarch.

All you saw was nothing, which was the same
as seeing everything. From within
that fluent perspective,

the only thought that occurred
(if what babies do can be equated to thinking):
*my mother is not here,*
*therefore, I am not here.*

And then maybe she'd lean forward,
and you'd catch a glimpse of her flared nostrils
or the fleshy chin, trembling.

Maybe a voice would accompany the vision—
yet, the matriarchal totems
seemingly favor a mute presence.

3.
Later I am thinking about this mutable relationship;
1 mother=2 grandmothers;
Naturally there is tension.

4.
The last time
my father took me to his childhood home
was when his mother died.

Her memorial service took place in July.

One day during our visit, my father took me and my cousins
to Mount Lassen—his idea of heaven, I suppose.

Despite the summer season and the
sticky heat below in the Sacramento River valley,
marbled snowbanks still loomed fifty feet above the road.
We slid down them on our buttocks,
my cousins and I, smiling.

And yet all I felt
was this unpleasant, heavy,
nearly indescribable sensation—
the body's attachments—

slow trundle of the pelvis
loose with hormones,
the gravity of its architraves,
its gothic vaults,
jeweled organ contained within,
its irresistible promise of *lux nova*,
white light shining behind
something swollen and blood-wired.

5.
During that same visit,
I heard my grandmother's voice
speaking to me one morning;
perhaps a durable sort
of music superimposed itself,
stung through with early apricots,
pomegranates, and the faint
rust of my grandfather's
long-abandoned farm tools.

6.
Now, fifteen years later,
the dogwood, the neon green
tips of the Douglas fir, like wardens,
beckon to me from beyond the threshold.

Is it the sky that wants me
or just my question, which points to nothing
beside itself?

7.
When my grandmother observed
the mountain beyond the orchards
stretching the eye to its dry margins,
perhaps she perceived its brilliance, its beauty;
perhaps both of which she considered no less than distraction.

My father perhaps perceived a memory of his own fear,
which in this case stands in for temptation,
the force of his own ambition.

When I see the mountain, I recognize
a faint shape carving into the sky,
but it is not a part of a face that
I've been taught to recognize.

(And who among the family,
upon seeing its silhouette,
conjured the memory of its mud pots,
the far-yellow stink of sulphur, and felt,
if only momentarily, blessed by their own life?)

8.
My grandmother's voice
arrived one long-ago
summer morning,
and has not returned to me since.

9.
Now, the approaching season calls out,
offers an alternative to assigning
those familiar, stable meanings:

You can pick the fallen fruit,
the unripe walnuts,
toxic in their green skins, or
you can let your hands fall to the side;
you can click the button,
you can close the need for this
labor of memory.

Then, you may lie
here for a little while longer,
belly to the ground.

10.

With the head turned—through
the crab grass,
maybe you witness
pairs of feet,
coming or going,
to where, who knows, suppose
the mountain scatters,
far beyond the margins,
those permitted angles.

## El Señor del Árbol
## (San Enrique de Velasco, Ecuador, 2016)

I never prayed to the man in the tree.
But I tasted his sap once in the altitudes.
And it was stringent and perfumed—
as if tinctured with aniseed and ozone.
Small amounts made the blood
rush in warm gyres
and provisioned lustrous clouds.

Men and women gathered
with offerings—freshly dug potatoes,
bags of rice, fruits, blankets, corn,
live chickens and plenty of Pájaro Azul.

We danced for him on the earth's navel,
passing cups of beer clockwise
in memory of his impassive expression
that encircled us like thorns.

For the man in the tree, the sin
was not the act, nor even the intent;
but rather in their subduction.

If I was guilty then—I was guilty of all three.

Meanwhile the hurricanes
played to the atmospheres
their refrain to tolerate more—more
of the ecstasy, more of the fracas,
more of the party for the wooden god—
all to soothe his apparent sorrow
at the ending of youth and the passage
of the rains into the next meridian.

+V+

## Yıldız/Star

The village suckles
a clay-fattened duct through the forest.
Beneath where it empties out in ruddy mounds,
an animalic sea looms.

And the smoke of burning leaves colors
the vision, littered
with shell scraps and manure.

In the evening the star wanders the pastures.
Lumbers amidst the houses,
heaving with old masonry and salt.

When I first took
the cow's udder in my small hands
the milk would not come easily. And yet I
pulled thin streaks of light in the evening sky
while she hummed into her oats.

Another day in the valley, the bell ringing
to signal the homecoming, the papillae pliant.
Above, the old mosque webs itself
into the world with electric cables
and concrete to gird its swelling wattles.

An auntie sweeps the patio and shoos the cats
away; the sun floats like cream,
licks sweet mouthfuls of light
across the breakfast tables and grasses.

In childhood we named them first:
the star, the cow, the glands:
one mute, one mellow, one favored—

yet their memory requires
the nourishment of sounds beyond
the hollow bell of the mother.

**Yoğurt**

Esra walks up the road carrying two plastic jugs full of milk.
Her solid figure describes the morning, edged
in by the fragrant mud of the damp fields.

The village moves slowly at the margins,
its mid-morning work, harnessed in
roils of rooster calls.

In counterpart, the ezan
stratifies the atmosphere with its austere beauty
at regular intervals.

Always the dogs reply.
The news of God's existence startles
and causes among them great commotion.
In between, they will forget about it
and return to their intricate worlds of scent.

The litany of orange cats threads its way along Esra's path,
curious as to which house she will make her stop. Can they
hope for a little saucerful?

Today she is going to Nedim Amca's green house on the hill.
It is hardly occupied anymore—only on occasion
when the old man or his sister come for a visit.
A funeral maybe, or to see the youngest brother,
the only sibling who stayed.

Esra knocks at the door, proffers the milk, and is invited in for tea,
But she must decline now—more of the day's work waits.

The youngest cat mews as Esra turns to leave,
and the morning's hoped-for milk appears.

In the evening, down at Aysel Yenge's, they will gather
to have tea, crack fresh walnuts, and catch up.

The wood stove will sputter its own stories,
and the children will run around, greet Nedim Amca,
whose eyes will shine at their antics.
Esra will play with the baby who lost her mother
in the accident, a year ago.

Meanwhile, Aysel Yenge will take her own portion of milk to the
kitchen and prepare fresh yogurt,
sparkling and sour,
conjured from the remains of last week's batch.
She will make yogurt soup with mint, ayran, and bread for the
guests.

After the meal, after the mirative,
Esra will return home with a portion of soup to share with her
mother-in-law.
She will call her son and remind him to repair the broken tiles.
She will take out the buckets of washing water
and splash their contents at the base of the plum trees,
which have just begun their delicate flowering.
She will then pause, to observe the
night's emergence:

The cobblestones, glimmering in announcement of moonrise
bushes rustling, yowling cats in heat.
The abandoned homes down the road slumping
a little further to the ground,
returning their memories as they dissolve
into Esra's long and steady breathing.

## Daphne in the Garden

*After Louise Glück*

*Woe to me, because love is curable by no herbs*
*nor the skills which benefit all benefit their master!*
*-Ovid, Metamorphoses*

1.
The garden table was lain,
replete with the gifts of the earth.

At the same time, its song was sewn shut
with the strings of Apollo's harp.

Beyond, the shallow refrain of my father's river;

I've called out for saving before—

he will not respond again,
nor will I owe him tribute.

2.
Behold:
all manner of cheeses:
tel peyniri, lor peyniri, Tulum peyniri, beyaz peyniri—
clustered together in
glistening globes, throbbing and pale
like embryos in the petri dish—
Beside them—olives from the orchard,
swimming in oil and brine;
breads, cucumbers, tomatoes, peppers,
honey, cream, molasses,
tahini, and butter:
everything you could wish for, of bounty.

Although the yellow jackets
do play a role in the banquet—
pay them no mind,

their gold-tipped arrows,
threatening with appetite.

Eros has already bestowed me
his leaden antidote.

You devour; I merely observe.

3.
The girl gathers in her thin limbs
boughs of laurel—
heavy and supple, like the carcass
of a hunted deer. She conveys them into
piles amidst streams of late spring
sunlight.

Blood pools in her womb
like expectation. Then
a flash of fever, urging her along
this pointless labor,
rooting her into the loam.

4.
No one can do anything about the mess
of the garden now. This foliage requires
the span of a summer to dry
before it can be burned.

There is no way to compete with it
'til autumn.

After that, the promised kiss,
then: winter's darkness.

5.
*If some things lie hidden,*
*she imagines them better.*

6.
There is no need to grieve now;
the laurel is hardy and will proliferate
at an alarming pace.

Take care to prune the branches
in the coming years,
not just this once,

lest they overwhelm you
with their monstrous, evergreen
future.

7.
Tell me, Eros,
what is your aim?
Sure, I understand the need
to prove oneself as a lesser god—
your means were questioned,
the grace of your weapons, scorned.

It is like you said:
even a man of such unprecedented beauty
can't control his own desire.

If the women aren't aware,
then perhaps someone should tell them.

But what did you want of
*my* suffering amidst *his* errors?

I was content, alone in the woods—
I was among the mammals and the mushrooms,
no one expected convention of me.

I tendered my own archery.

Prophecy held no meaning then—

neither fear, nor expectation,
nor ambition.

No one thought to warn me of these things;
even I thought I knew myself.

I was quick before these roots took hold.
I ran swiftly; do you remember me that way?

And still, you admire how deftly
I shudder and shrink before you;
how even this heavy
curse cannot fully bind me.

8.
I gathered the laurels
around my body;
I adorned my head with their horns
as if to shield myself
from knowledge of loss.

What good is it to lament that
which no one will miss?

Knots of human tissue, knots of desire—
pulsing through,
numbing the exits—

these, the animal dreams
of the unborn,
escaping through me,
yielding to some
alternative divinity.

9.
Later, in the market—the selection of fresh cheeses:
curds, sandwiches, pastas;
your friends were there, and I

entertained it all—
a good sporting.

From time to time—
thick clots passing between my legs,
thesis of human life
without form;

a discharge of possibility,
a plumb line tracing us to
this imagined feast, lain before the victors.

10.
Did you not say *we kiss before we burn*?
I recall your taste—metallic and pure,
your quivering flesh—

I sought refuge from your splendor,
untouchable, even now.

So, I will announce your victory
at the Pythian Games.

11.
And who is it that burns among us?
Victor or vanquished?

Don't ask me to speak anymore;
I'll crown whoever pleases me
and privately mourn
the players
all equally
*in ransom—your emblem—*

## Carnophallogoscentrism

A.
If the animal is blue, it is said to symbolize
the sky, or a wish for the sky—
    i.     birds understood this assignment,
    ii.    and some reptiles, many insects. Mammals
on the other hand, cling with their furs
the comfort of earth (or is it
the other way around?)
    iii.   A human would be permitted to eat the sky, anyway,
           if sky assumed the identity of meat, or that of a phallus,
        1. in order to fulfill its presumed duty to itself as species
sovereign.

B.
The body is not human,
nor is it inhabited by an identity
that can be reduced to a singularity;
    i.     nothing unique is contained fully
           within the flesh;
        1. Exhibit: flakes of dead skin
           sloughing off in the wind,
        2. Exhibit: in the rustling together of forms
              a. nothing is missed,
              b. no crisis emerges
              c. when the tongue licks
              d. and takes you with it
C.
Along the rows of steel crates—
clicking of claws, a sign for speech
that makes no discernable meaning
of itself.
    i.     Meanwhile, the human observers cluster
           in the far corners,
           and exercise their primate rituals, their fawning,
           their baring of teeth,
              1. Exhibit: the teasing question of whether

a blue-painted wall will calm the group.
2. Then, they are permitted
ii. to devour the lower in rank, mere animals—
an act coeval with fulfillment—
iii. the trajectory of life and death—
iv. none of which is embodied, but rather prescribed,
in a sense, as antidote,
1. its sky notions braying the telomeres.

D.
In the blue-painted room—
sound of a zipper, like a bell ringing;
i. Exhibit: salivation
ii. one body kneeling before another,
iii. so familiar it is with the cost of subjugating the
body as separate in its particular species of desire
a. as something that rises and falls, insisting
b. it will
elide its own animal perception;

E.
and the blue wall
i. bends through it.

**Late Spring**

All spring I watched the garden
roar its way through the confusion of seasonal affect
and refused to intervene—

The fallen laurel branches from last season
continued their ritual of memento mori in slow motion
beside the piles of apple and cherry branches
lain along the fenceline like rotten roses at an abandoned shrine.

At times I felt the urge to collect it all in my arms—
this detritus—and relegate it to the further edges
where nothing substantial spores the shade with novelty,
but each time the thought occurred to me,
I dismissed it and resumed my suffering.

Something familiar must steady the passage of time.

Now I watch the burgeoning foxgloves with fascination,
unfolding their palms to each new day
as if faith were the only answer.

I remind myself—had I taken to the
weeding dutifully in March,
I would have extirpated their promise,
not knowing what they were, one thing vs. another,
unable to appreciate the course of
their spackled, purple futures hollowing out
the air like optic nerves connecting
eyeballs to some monstrous, vegetal brain.

In their sheer muscle I perceive
the fragmented image of a man I saw running yesterday,
along the busy road. He wasn't running, really,
but striding confidently, as if he were cooling
down from a twenty-miler, camelback strapped
across his bare chest like artillery, his lean body

rippling with endorphins, sweat seeping
along the brown neck, his fragile joints
adorned with the raiments of well-calibrated
hamstrings and quadriceps—

these were the kind of things
I once placed my faith in, before my body
began to live out its own purpose separately from me.
Yet the lure is still present—beauty and strength—
isn't there freedom in those, if only tended properly,
when one immerses oneself in their incremental ceaselessness?

My days now are subsumed by other routines,
as if the mind must persist according to some ideal of itself,
even if it can never fully occupy the human form—

still, it keeps its habits:
the morning, the workday, then sleep—
the messes accumulating and dispersing accordingly,
awareness of children anchoring
any sense of time into what it perceives
to be limbs—no church, no tools—
swinging thoughts as if thoughts were more than vapors,
intoxicating, transient—
as if they were cultivars, something that can
feed another living thing.

And as with the garden, I must eventually
step back, let the mind have its way until
it no longer regards me as a suspicious stranger,
ready to knock down whatever
returns the sign of its
own strength to the tyranny of seasons.

## Miss Rachel is My Hero

The moon tonight—
dim like a dirty coin fished
from the pockets
of a dead woman's jacket.

Yet, she still feeds us
the blinding brilliance of
another, far away
explosion.

Elsewhere:
a mother who does not
eat cannot nurse
her children.

Refusal is refusal.

A denial is also denial.

Until it becomes that
last acknowledged desire:
only to absorb what is given,
never to pronounce it
with our own mouths,
to always muffle and confuse the consonants.

Broken lines between
past and present
are not the only consequence;
it is the angles,
relations themselves—

that which describes the trajectory:

One body refracting
through the Euclidean silence of
another.

## Watering the Garden in May

The sky is uncharacteristically hazy today—
as if the atmosphere were stuffed with gauze
to close the blaring wound of sunlight,
an urgent yet languorous rescue of transitions.

A nitrile blue semaphore
slips its signal under a veil of invisible particles,
swirls the blood cells in the capillaries—pale
and completely bleached of necessity, of metals—

pale, like an afternoon in late summer, when the fires
have already bloomed in the forests,
and the mountains to the east threaten
the softness of your red leisure with
fangs of glinting wilderness.

But it is not summer today, only late spring.
The rhododendrons are in full tachycardic spawn
(furious fuchsia hearts) and
sugar ants resume their feasting conquests.
No matter what I do to stem the encroachment,
they insist in favor of their own inexorable nature,
not mine.

In the garden my daughter fills a hole
with water from the hose,
her hair falling around her
as she concentrates
on the clear chord of water. She holds
the bright green hose over this hole,
which appears to be quite shallow.

For a long time, the water arches
along a pure trace of gravity, and yet the hole
does not overflow.

I observe her at her work, and through my observation
attempt to sink deeply
with each impression into the impossible present:

the body, after all, must maintain its finitudes.

Amidst the chatter of bluebirds and juncos
cutting into the blurring ripples of last night's medicines
swarming my synapses:
I sense I am losing hold of something,
a meaning for which no sign ever revealed itself.

Is this the feeling of vitality slipping away, as if
I've surrendered to consensus reality, finally,
all I had to offer it?

As if it has leached memory from me
for its own structure, like
calcium from a femur,
a casually rotten lintel that threatens collapse,
though it be only one
among so many as to be inconsequential?

My mind pinches like the walls
of the hose around this question.

Whatever else runs through it—
pouring into the space where possibility
once existed: it now recedes into a
hole in time.

And it occurs to me: that hole in time is the earth—
or it is my own body—or it is nothing
that can be measured in substance—
element by element sinking
into the space where some awareness,.
some alien effort,
left no clue as to its jurisdiction.

## Wean

*After Søren Kierkegaard and Rina Swentzell*

1.
It is tempting to consider
the world as liberation.
Its sanguine hopes—folded
within the cyanide shadows
billowing in the trees,
the tail of the sun
rippling into each
grain along the shore.

The best of us
sleep within the ice
of its neglect.

Meanwhile, we do gut
the ground,
seeking out mineral seed
with which to sow
our own idol hunger.

This act of selection,
it ages us into obedience—

and it draws the knife—

2.
When they built the first earthen dwellings
the women gathered around the walls
to taste its many-colored clays,
to remember—

3.
What it meant to quit the liquids of the earth—
where you swam, suspended in artless rapture.

You,
consciousness before boundary,
the lipids snared in
the idea of the body
as extension,
as first appendage—
a pulp of accidents.
I was there, then, as you insist—

illuminated in the gestalt of the first oceans.
And, like you
in your time,
I arranged all aspects of the self
like a squid that both contains and is contained by
the premise of its own ink.

4.
Familied molecules rolled in unison—
the system, whole,
the bowl, full

all life subsumed—
the Platonic law, universal
and thus horizonless.

The star yet did not rise
on its own shores.

It savored the bitumen
of the scorched heavens,
like a babe latched
into its simple vacuum
where it knew only shallow comfort.

5.
Was this tenderness—your first gesture beyond the flagrant
pleasure of the fumaroles, piercing

into darkness, an exodus, which you ventured
not as one driven by absence *of*
but rather by satiety *within*

as you were borne up by the unnamed agency
we now acknowledge as breath?

Then, innocent stripes of an alien light sculpted
orbs into your awareness

and the obedient tongue laps
at the wet shores.

6.
When you turn your breast away from the infant
you briefly recall the first, miraculous
emergence on the black rocks.

The head—knowing itself for the first time
as the highest point,
its pulsating
rhythms now lost
in the strange winds of language.

Above the lip of your being, the muscles
struggling into endless ellipse, somewhere
less than synchronicity—their
absurd attempts to provide
the rudiments of movement,
balancing the delicious patagia,
the spongy and the osseous spindles
erected into
efficient pursuit;

these coordinations
that come to find
their clearest expression in the ruthless—
those men of perfect faith.

Yes, they could kill a son
and so forget the praise of currents.

7.
When the windstorm swept through yesterday,
the power went out.

This morning, a fog descended,
then a frost descended,
pure
like information.

In the afternoon,
the temperatures will rise
and swim the ripe air.

The night will behold
the chittering of black crickets,
the visions—
finally expelled.

And yet we drink it,
the noise of the earth—
its lakes of routine,
its gargled verbs
throating heavily in the dream-straw.

8.
I creatured myself into your body,
and when your body changed
I could no longer
understand you.

Concealed in the first ocean,
you disappeared beyond the milky tongue
furred with yeast
and so forgot the meaning of my hunger.

9.
Did I survive you?

If this rooting
can be called surviving,
if it can be called
to satisfaction—

10.
Observe, now:
the earth provisions
stronger food at hand.

Ambitious starches, thickets
of blood-threaded berries,
apples purled with buttery grubs,
clasps of golden grasses
that sing the rain machines,
the silvery fangs of olives,
the fawning, errant figs,
mineral tangs of dirts
sculpting their own hands
into containers and ovens and homes
to lend softness to
the beans and breads—

all so that the child will not perish.

11.
Though the sorrow is indeed immense—

great fortune
of the black earth,

it turns away.

## Endnotes

The lines "De día y de noche/quisiera tomar mi tetita" from the epigraph are lyrics from Peruvian folklore singer, Wendy Sulca's, hit song, "La Tetita."

In "Origins" the line "çeşme başında" is Turkish for "at the fountain," which comes from a song, "Perşembe Günüde Çeşme Başında." Here it is intended to be textural, or heard as if from a distance, and unclearly, threading through the voice of the poem.

In "Placentae" the reference to the bell comes from a film by Andrei Tarkosvsky, *Andrei Rublev* (1966). In the film the workmen do not starve but are successful in their work.

In "Let Down Reflex" *Ammonoidea* refer to extinct, coiled-shelled cephalopods whose fossils, referred to as "snakestones," were thought to be evidence of the actions of saints in medieval England.

In her poem "My Head and My Mother's Breast in Quarantine Together" from the collection, *Balladz* (Knopf, 2022), Sharon Olds references the ancient English word for dragon was *worme*, spelled as it appears in the poem here, "Colostrum."

The lines "Sóplame un canto sencillo y duradero" and "Comadrona de mil nudos" come from a poem by Adriana Paredes Pinda, "Machi Adriana Paredes Pinda-PM #5. Festival Poesía y Música BíoBío," poetry Reading January 2022, posted September 2022, 10 min, 31 sec., https://www.youtube.com/watch?v=c_Bu9KkH998.

The *Madonna Lactans* (also referred to as Nuestra Señora de la Leche or Nuestra Señora de Belén in Spanish) was an iconographical type featuring Mary breastfeeding her son. In Bethlehem there is a famous grotto with stones that are said to have turned white after some of the Virgin's milk dripped on the rocks. Women would mix these stones, which had high levels of calcium carbonate, with water, producing a milky-colored liquid that was said to assure a plentiful milk supply. The iconography of the nursing Madonna has very old origins within Christian church and traveled to the Americas following the Spanish conquest.

Mateo Pérez de Alesio (b. 1547-d.1616) was a painter of Southern Italian origin who is considered an influential figure in the development of Christian painting in colonial Peru following his immigration there in the late 16th century. See Francisco Stastny, "Pérez de Alesio y la pintura del siglo XVI," *Anales del Instituto de Arte Americano y de Investigaciones Estéticas* 22 (Buenos Aires, 1969): 69-84. He, like many artists working in the colonial Andes, used natural pigments derived from minerals, precious materials, stones, insects, and vegetal sources.

"The Apparition of the Virgin to Saint Bernard" refers to the hagiographical account of the *Lactatio Bernardi* miracle of Saint Bernard of Clairvaux (b. 1090-d. 1153), the co-founder of the Knights Templar and the father of the Cistercian Order of Benedictines, who was said to have received the favor of the Virgin Mary when she sprayed some of her milk in his eyes—some accounts say that the drops fell on his lips—while asleep or deep in prayer.

When babies have eye infections, breast milk is an effective remedy.

Bartolomé Esteban Murillo (b.1617-d.1682) was a highly prolific and popular Spanish Baroque painter whose work is often associated with the counterreformation era.

Ascites refers to a buildup of fluid in the belly due to cancer, organ failure, tuberculosis, and several other diseases. When a person has ascites, their belly will swell, making the person appear to be pregnant.

In the poem "Bilirubin," the reference to Luci Tapahonso is in honor of her poem, "Old Salt Woman" from *A Radiant Curve* (University of Arizona Press, 2008), which describes the origin of the Navajo (Diné) ceremony for a baby's first laugh, in which relatives gather to celebrate a baby after they laugh for the first time. The baby shares salt with everyone in memory of Old Salt Woman. The lines in the same poem, "me sube la bilirrubina/cuando te miro y no me miras," come from a song by Juan Luis Guerra, "La Bilirrubina."

"El Señor del Árbol" refers to a miraculous image of Jesus that appeared near the church near San Antonio de Pichincha (in modern-day Ecuador) in a quishuar tree, a tree which has spiritual significance in pre-Colonial Andean culture.

The ezan refers to the call to prayer in "Yoğurt." Ayran is a popular Turkish drink made from yogurt, salt, and water. The word, "yogurt" itself is Turkish in origin.

The poem, "Daphne in the Garden," builds on Louise Glück's "Mythic Fragment" from *The Triumph of Achilles* (Ecco Press, 1985).

"Carnophallogoscentrism" refers to Jacques Derrida's idea that the act of eating meat reflects the dominance of male-centric discourse in *The Animal That I Therefore Am*, translated by Marie-Louise Mallet (Fordham University Press, 2008). The poem also evokes the color blue as it relates to the animal conscience, in reference to the literature of Suniti Namjoshi, as discussed by Samrita Sengupta Sinha in "The Decolonization of Queer Politics in Suniti Namjoshi's Select Animal Fables: Locating 'The Animal That I Therefore Am,' *Postcolonial Text* 20, no. 2 (2025): 1-18.

Miss Rachel has been vocal about her opposition to the genocide in Gaza, articulating what many of us are unable to—or are afraid to—say out loud. She also teaches toddlers how to talk and sing.

The poem, "Wean," references the first passages from Søren Kierkegaard's *Fear and Trembling* (published on October 16th, 1843), which features a poetic meditation on faith through the image of weaning an infant. The lines from section 2 of this poem also references Rina Swentzell's essay, "An Understated Sacredness," *MASS: Journal of the School of Architecture and Planning, University of New Mexico* (Fall 1985), in which she recalls tasting the adobe walls of the buildings as a child growing up in Santa Clara Pueblo (Kha'P'o Owinge).

## Acknowledgements

Thank you to the following publications where some of these poems are published/forthcoming:

*Amethyst Review*, "Madonna Lactans", Fall 2025

*Arcturus*, "Bilirubin" and "Yıldız/Star", Fall 2025

*Cathexis Northwest*, "General Anesthesia", May 2025

*HamLit*, "El Señor del Árbol (San Enrique de Velasco, Ecuador, 2016)", Summer 2025

*Flat Ink*, "Placentae", "Ascites", and "Memorial (For Martha)", Fall 2025

*Four Tulips*, "Early Spring" and "Risperidone", Spring 2025

*Neologism*, "Late Spring", Spring 2026

*Paraselene*, "The Amethyst", Spring 2025

*Thimble Literary Magazine*, "Colostrum", Fall 2025

*Trace Fossils*, "Swallow," 2024

Thank you to my teachers, both living and deceased, human, animal, and mineral.

I am thankful for the places where I wrote these poems—the ancestral lands of the Nisqually, Cowlitz, and Squaxin Island people, whose lands were forcibly removed and settled by generations of invaders. May the poetic urge allow us to name and honor the care for stories, the land, spirits, and knowledge that Indigenous peoples have advanced through millennia. May we know ourselves as part of this story. In my mind and heart are the histories, complicities, griefs, and joys that inhabit the Americas.

In memory of the children suffering from forced starvation and genocide. All children deserve nourishment, love, and protection.

## ABOUT THE AUTHOR

**Sonya Wohletz** is a writer whose work has appeared in Latin American Literary Review, Blue Unicorn, Amethyst Review, Roanoke Review, and others. Her first collection of poetry, *One Row After/Bir Sıra Sonra,* was published by First Matter Press in 2022.

## ABOUT THE PRESS

**South Broadway Press**
is a publisher of poetry through books, print journals, and on our online journal.

### OUR MISSION

Our mission is to provide a platform through poetry, writing, and art for ideas that provide alternatives to the harmful systems and ideologies that we historically have and continue to live among. We are interested in work that points us towards symbiosis with not just other humans, but with all beings in this moment, all beings past, and those future beings that will be impacted by the choices we collectively, and individually, make today. We focus our attention on love as a guiding force. Not a love that only reactively supports those who have been afflicted by oppression, but a love that is willing to disrupt, disobey, and proactively prevent and redirect the potential forthcoming affliction around us. A love that is resolute in its boundaries for itself and others. A love that takes the form of dissent, resistance, and in the words of John Lewis, a love that is willing to "get into good trouble".

**OUR SEAL**

Our seal is **the Bear, the Wrench, and the Quill.**

**The Bear** as a symbol of balancing softness with strength. The Bear as a call to approaching the caves of our internal worlds with curiosity. To slow living, and to laying witness to ourselves as not just material beings walking this Earth, but celestial beings, such as the great bear that graces the winter sky above us.

**The Wrench** as a symbol of disruption. A willingness to throw a wrench into the gears of fascism.

**The Quill** as a reminder of the adage that "the pen is mightier than the sword", and a calling to approach our work and play with that integrity and power in mind.

Our seal is also a nod to **Mutiny Information Cafe**, a bookstore, coffee shop, and community hub for over ten years now. A space that has time and again proved home for the cultivation of revolutionary ideas and the soft hearts that hold them.

www.ingramcontent.com/pod-product-compliance
Lightning Source LLC
LaVergne TN
LVHW051009080826
845145LV00009B/2536

* 9 7 8 1 7 3 5 0 3 5 5 6 7 *